FOR ORGANS, PIANOS & ELECTRONIC KEYBOARDS

E-Z PLAY TODAY

307

Gospel Songs
with 3 Chords

T0066616

ISBN 978-1-4234-8811-8

7777 W. BLUEMOUND RD. P.O. BOX 13819 MILWAUKEE, WI 53213

E-Z Play® Today Music Notation © 1975 by HAL LEONARD CORPORATION

E-Z PLAY and EASY ELECTRONIC KEYBOARD MUSIC are registered trademarks of HAL LEONARD CORPORATION.

Visit Hal Leonard Online at
www.halleonard.com

Contents

Beulah Land

Registration 3
Rhythm: Waltz

Words by Edgar Page Stites
Music by John R. Sweney

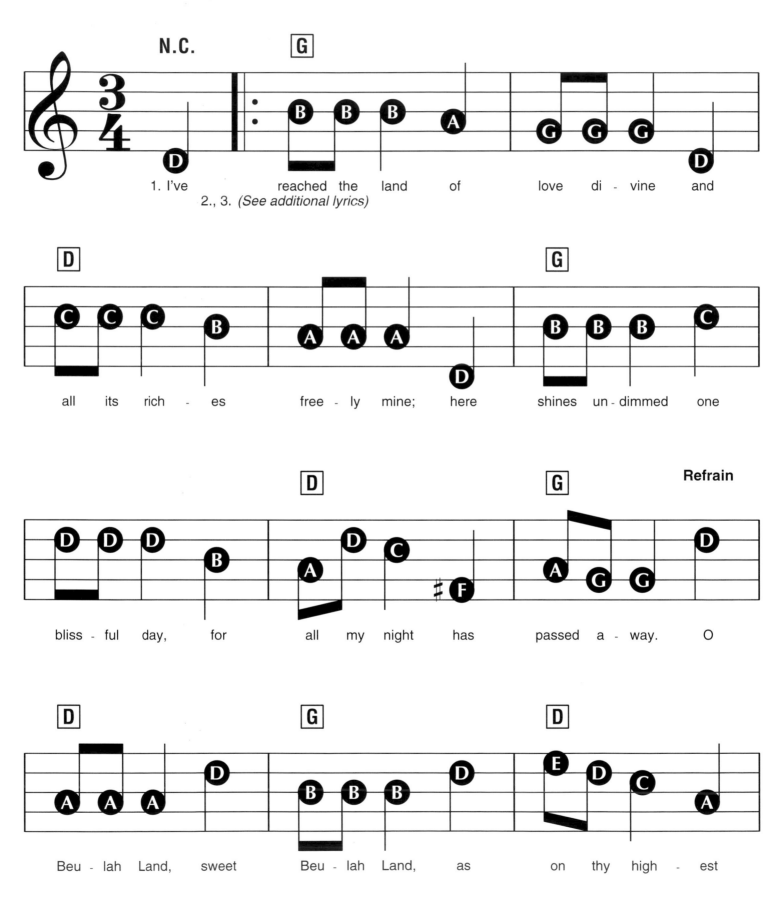

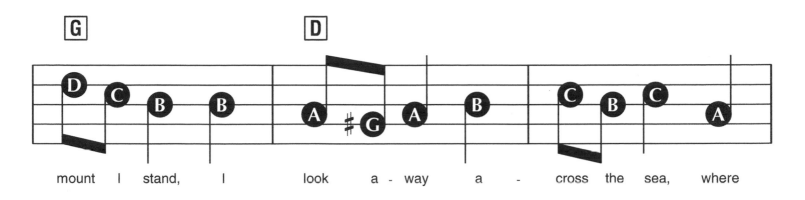

mount I stand, I look a - way a - cross the sea, where

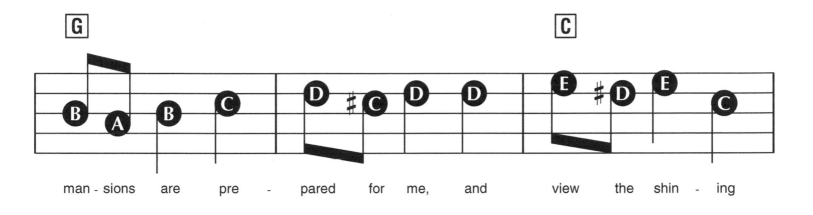

man - sions are pre - pared for me, and view the shin - ing

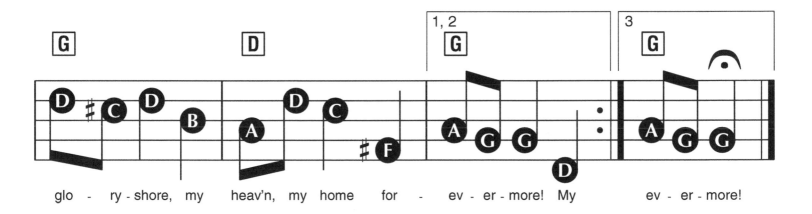

glo - ry - shore, my heav'n, my home for - ev - er - more! My ev - er - more!

Additional Lyrics

2. My Savior comes and walks with me,
   And sweet communion here have we;
   He gently leads me by His hand,
   For this is heaven's borderland.
   Refrain

3. The zephyrs seem to float to me,
   Sweet sounds of heaven's melody,
   As angels with the white-robed throng
   Join in the sweet Redemption song.
   Refrain

Down at the Cross
(Glory to His Name)

Registration 7
Rhythm: Country or Swing

Words by Elisha A. Hoffman
Music by John H. Stockton

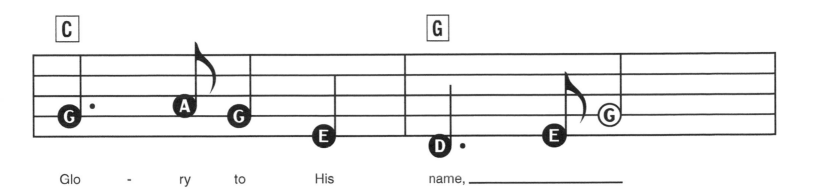

Glo - ry to His name, _____

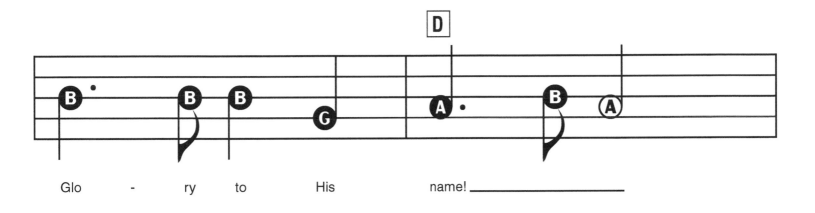

Glo - ry to His name! _____

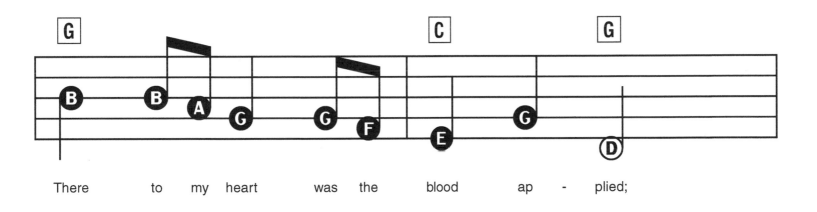

There to my heart was the blood ap - plied;

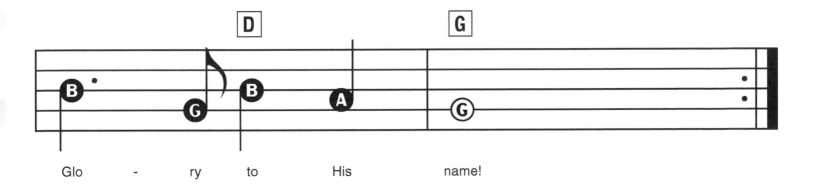

Glo - ry to His name!

The Eastern Gate

Registration 3
Rhythm: Fox Trot or Country

Words and Music by
Isaiah G. Martin

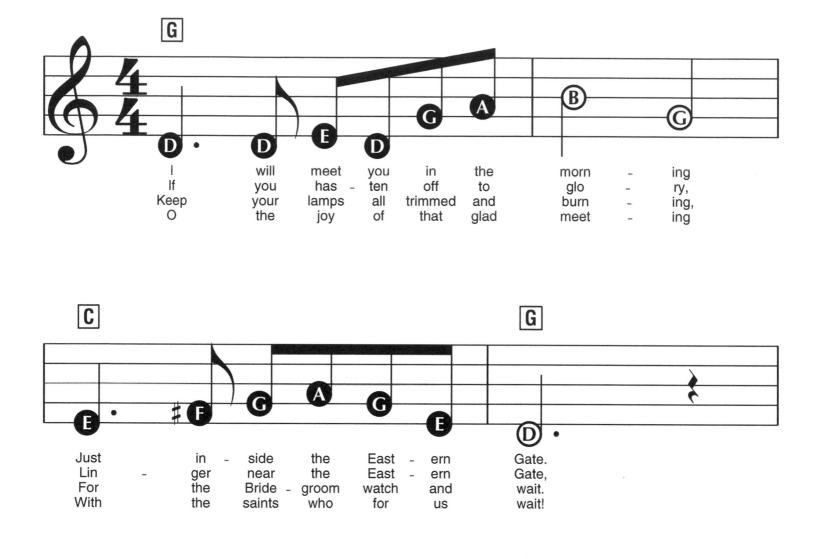

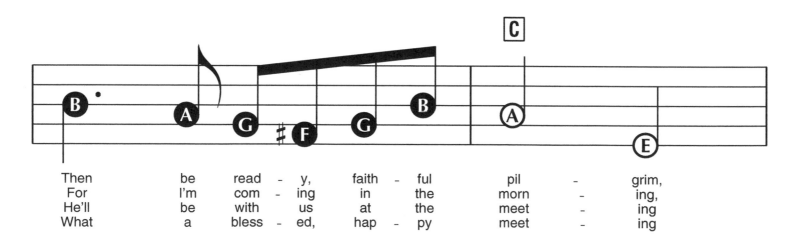

9

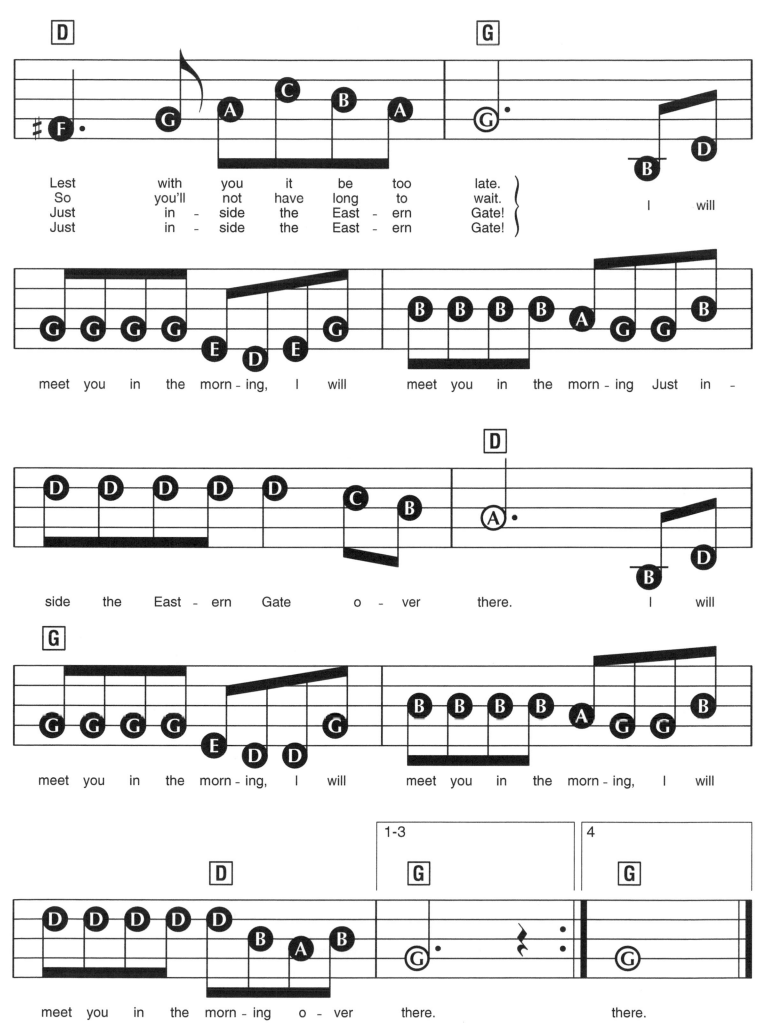

Every Day with Jesus

Registration 8
Rhythm: Fox Trot or Country

Words and Music by Robert C. Loveless
and Wendell P. Loveless

F — C

C D E F A A A C B C B C B ♭B

Ev - 'ry day with Je - sus is sweet - er than the day be - fore.

F

C D E G ♭B ♭B B ♭B C ♭B G ♯G A

Ev - 'ry day with Je - sus, I love Him more and more.

B♭

C D E F A A A C B C B C ♯C D

Je - sus saves and keeps me, and He's the One I'm wait - ing for.

F — C — F

D D F G A C A ♭B C ♭B C A G F

Ev - 'ry day with Je - sus is sweet - er than the day be - fore.

Farther Along

Registration 10
Rhythm: Waltz

Words and Music by J.R. Baxter, Jr.
and W.B. Stevens

N.C.   **F**

A   C   A   F   A

Tempt - ed	and	tried		we're
come				and
death				said
Je		-		sus

Bb   **F**

G   F   G   F   F

oft	made	to	won	-	der,
tak -	en	our	loved		ones,
our	lov -	ing	Mas	-	ter,
com -	ing	in	glo	-	ry,

A   C   D   C   A

why	it	should	be	thus
it	leaves	our	home	so
a	few	more	days	to
when	He	comes	from	His

C

A   G   F   G

all	the	day	long. _____
lone -	ly	and	drear. _____
la -	bor	and	wait. _____
home	in	the	sky. _____

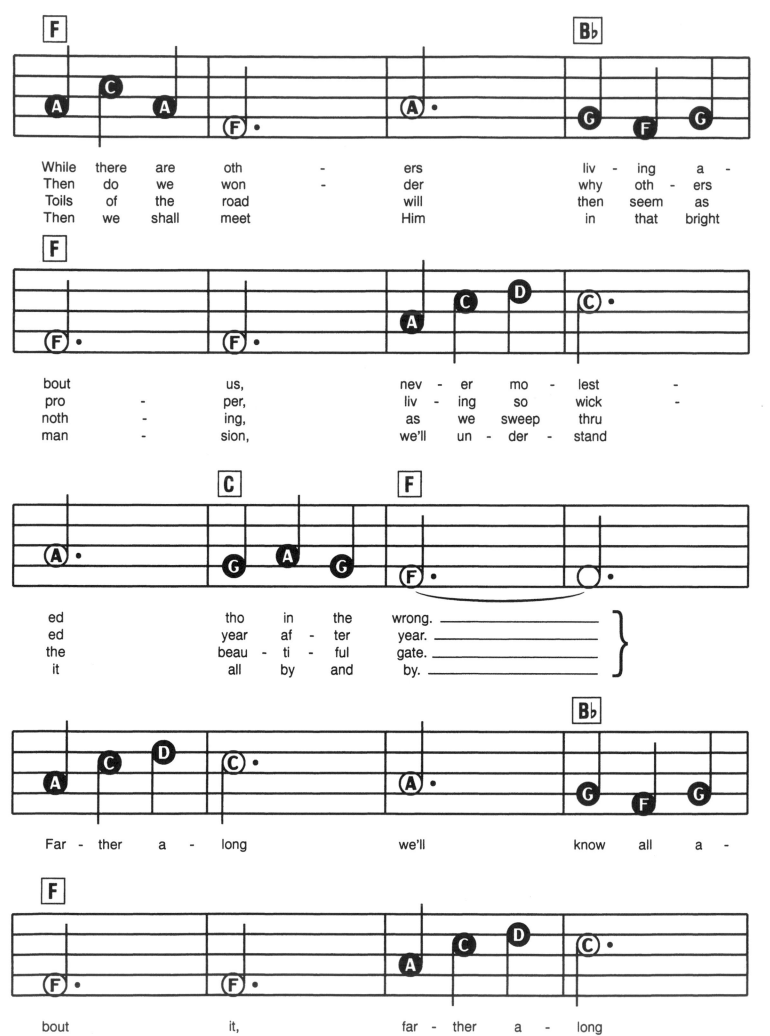

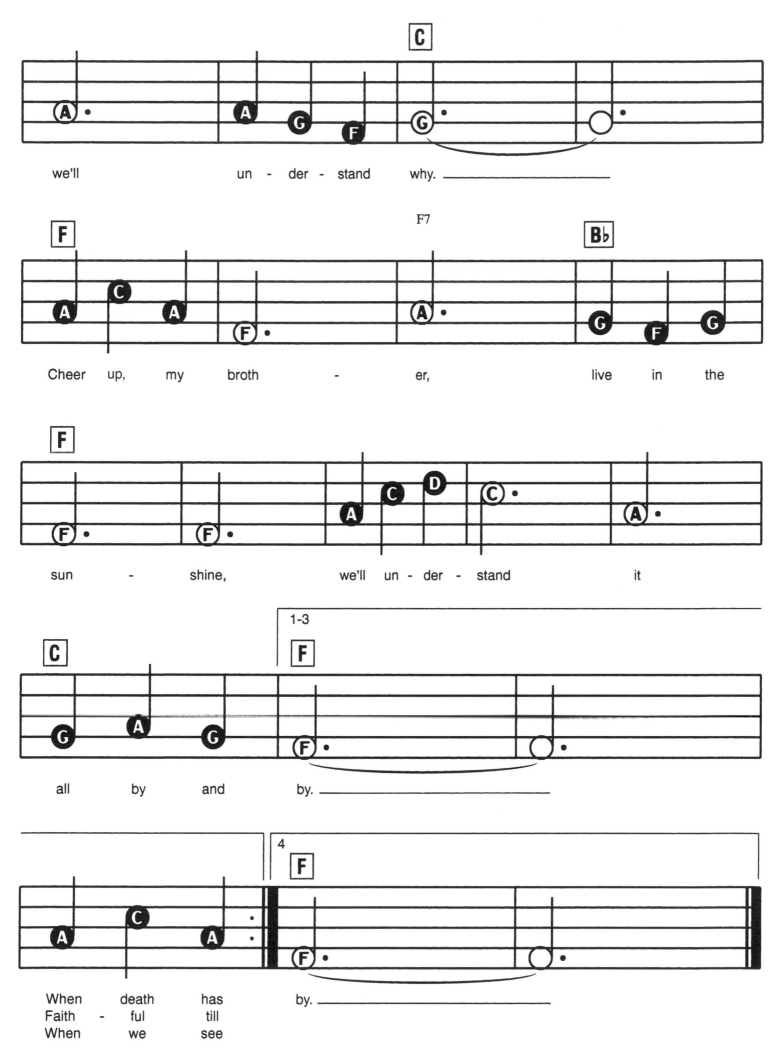

Heavenly Sunlight

Registration 2
Rhythm: Ballad

Words by Henry J. Zelley
Music by George Harrison Cook

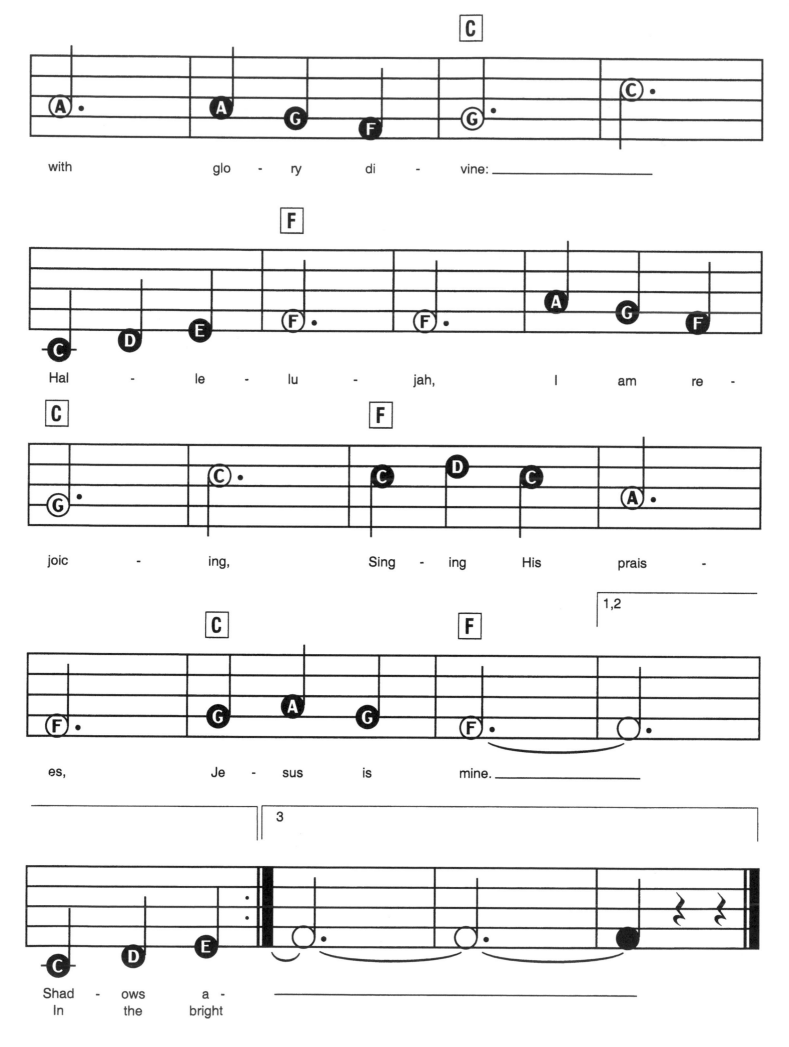

I Wouldn't Take Nothing for My Journey Now

Registration 4
Rhythm: Fox Trot or Country

Words and Music by Jimmie Davis
and Charles F. Goodman

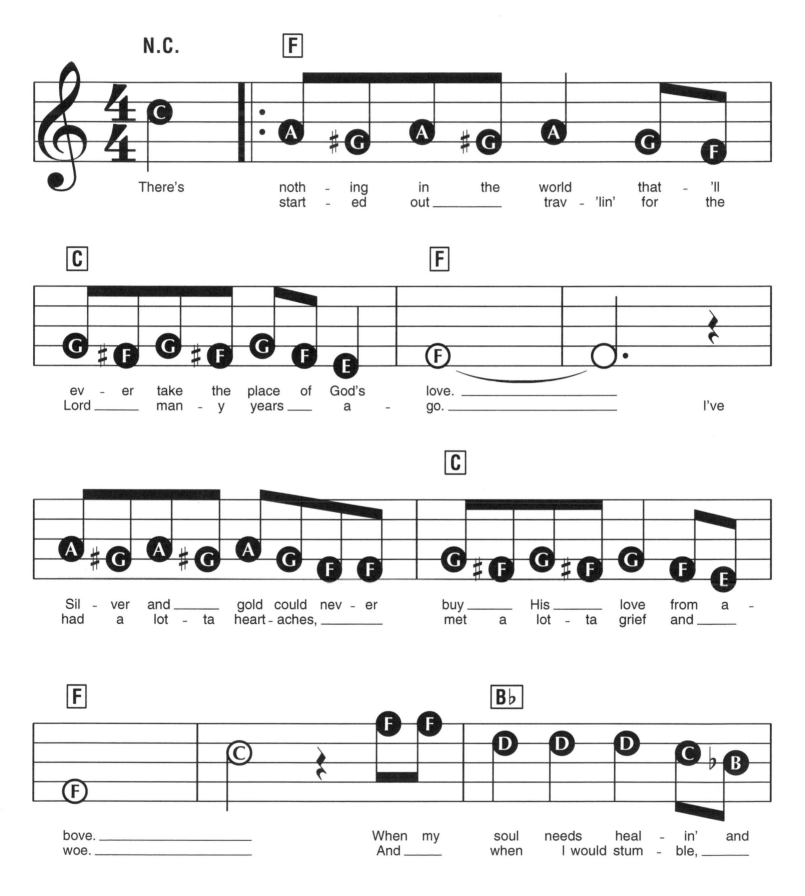

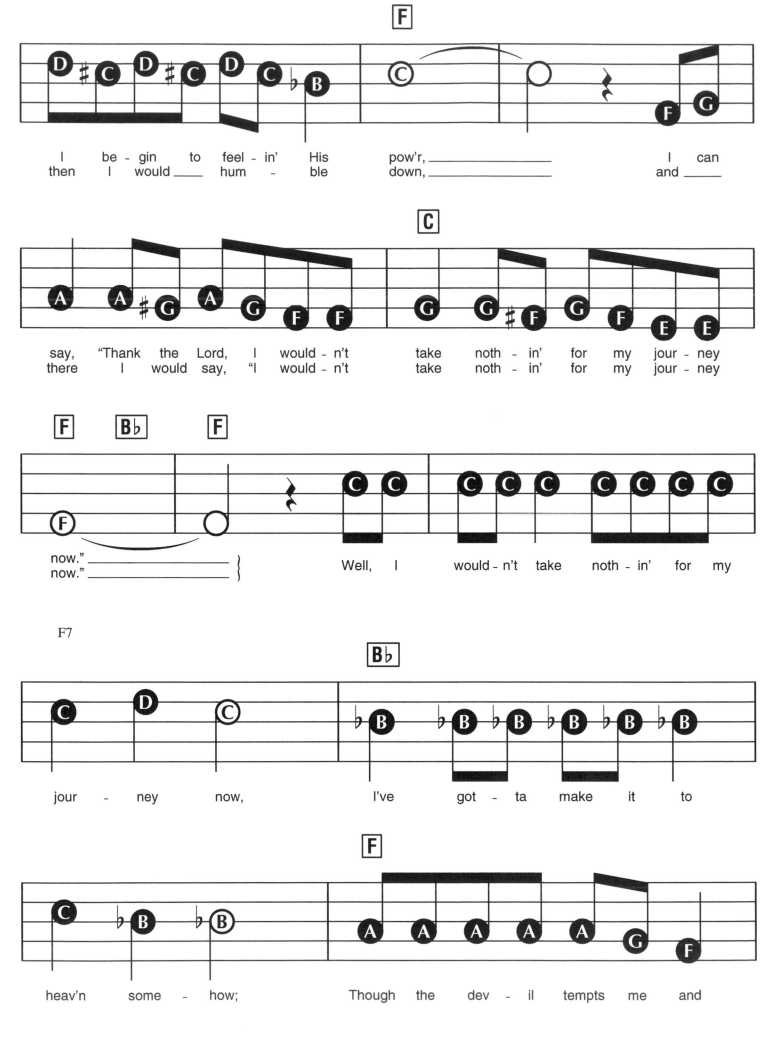

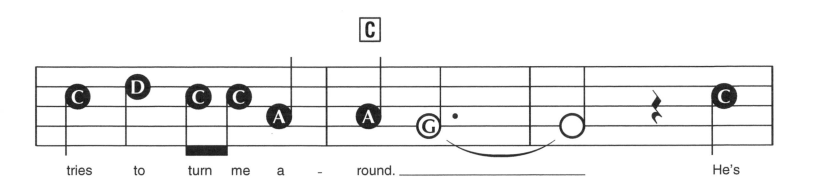

tries   to   turn   me   a - round. _____ He's

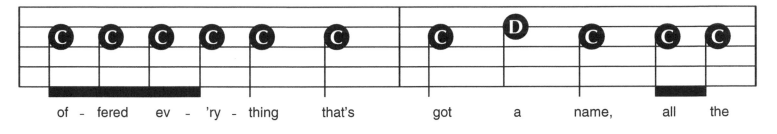

of - fered   ev - 'ry - thing   that's   got   a   name,   all   the

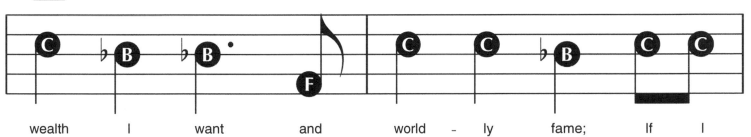

wealth   I   want   and   world - ly   fame;   If   I

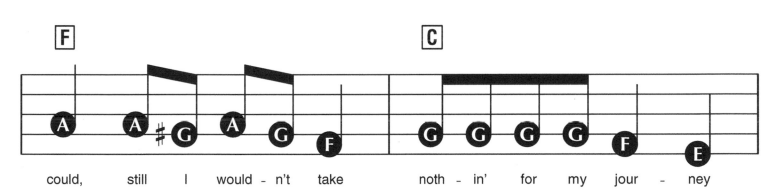

could,   still   I   would - n't   take   noth - in'   for   my   jour - ney

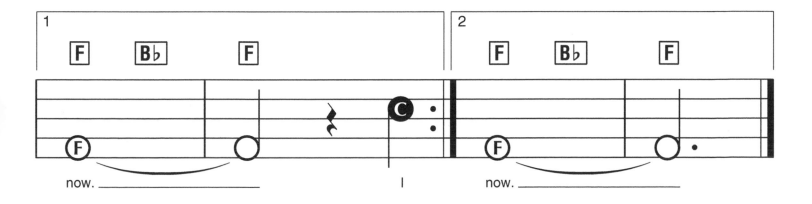

now. _____   I   now. _____

A Home in Heaven

Registration 2
Rhythm: Waltz

Words and Music by
Hank Williams

A - round me man - y are
Long is the road _____ that
read - y for _____ His

build - ing _____
leads you _____
com - ing, _____

To that homes of
beau - ti - ful
have you been

beau - ty and wealth, _____
home _____ up there. _____
true all a - long? _____

But what of a
Is work on your
Have you fin - ished your

home in Heav - en? _____
home com - plet - ed? _____
build - ing in Glo - ry, _____ will you

Where will you
Death may be
move to your

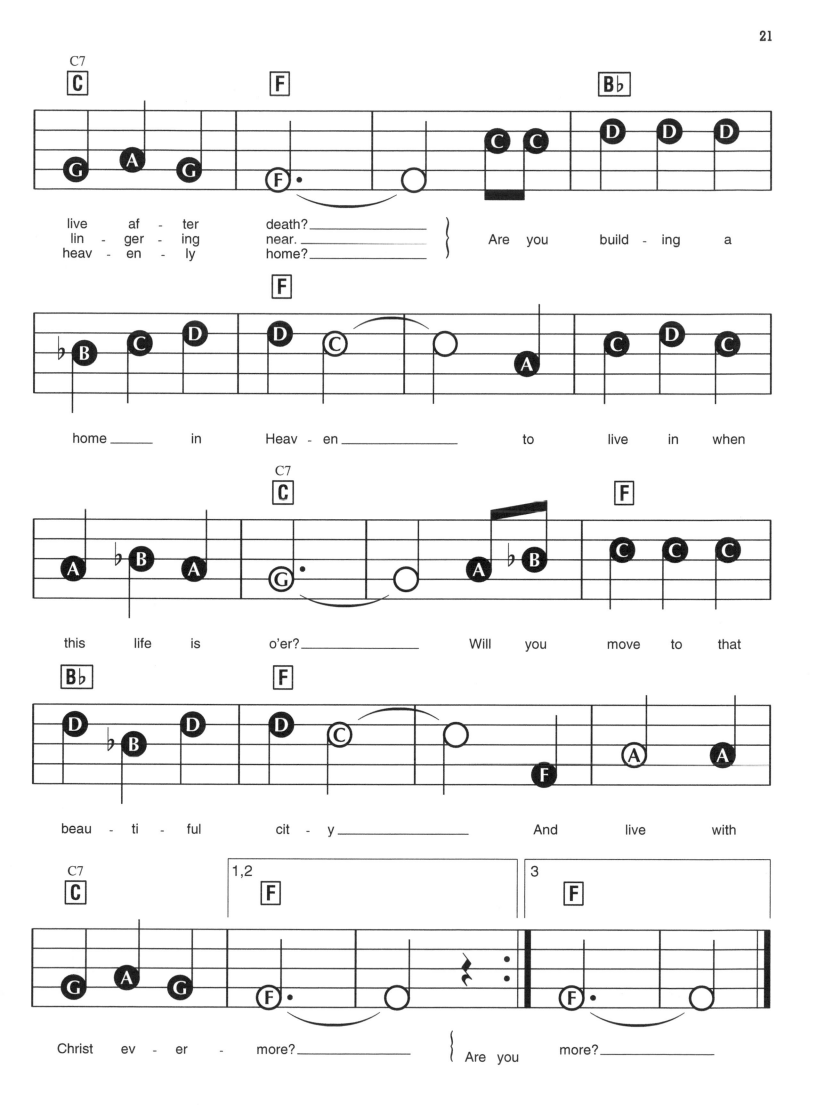

I Know a Man Who Can

Registration 8
Rhythm: Waltz

Words and Music by Jimmie Davis
and Jack Campbell

Invisible Hands

Registration 3
Rhythm: Waltz

Words and Music by Francis Stanton,
Buddy Kaye, Frederick Patrick and William Harrington

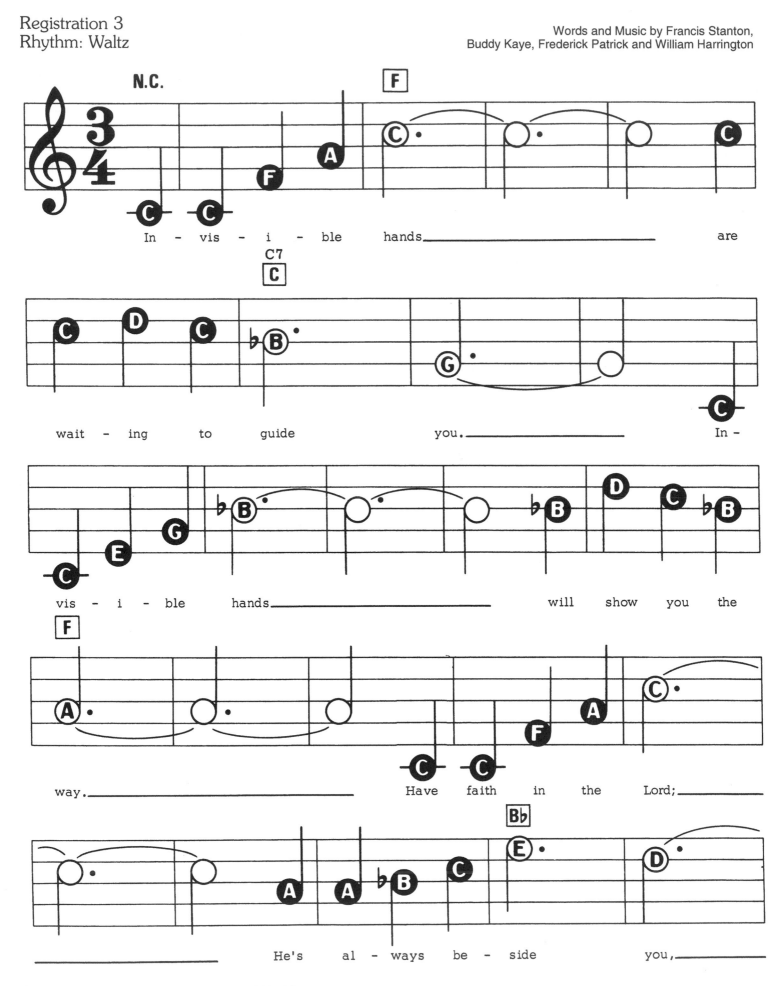

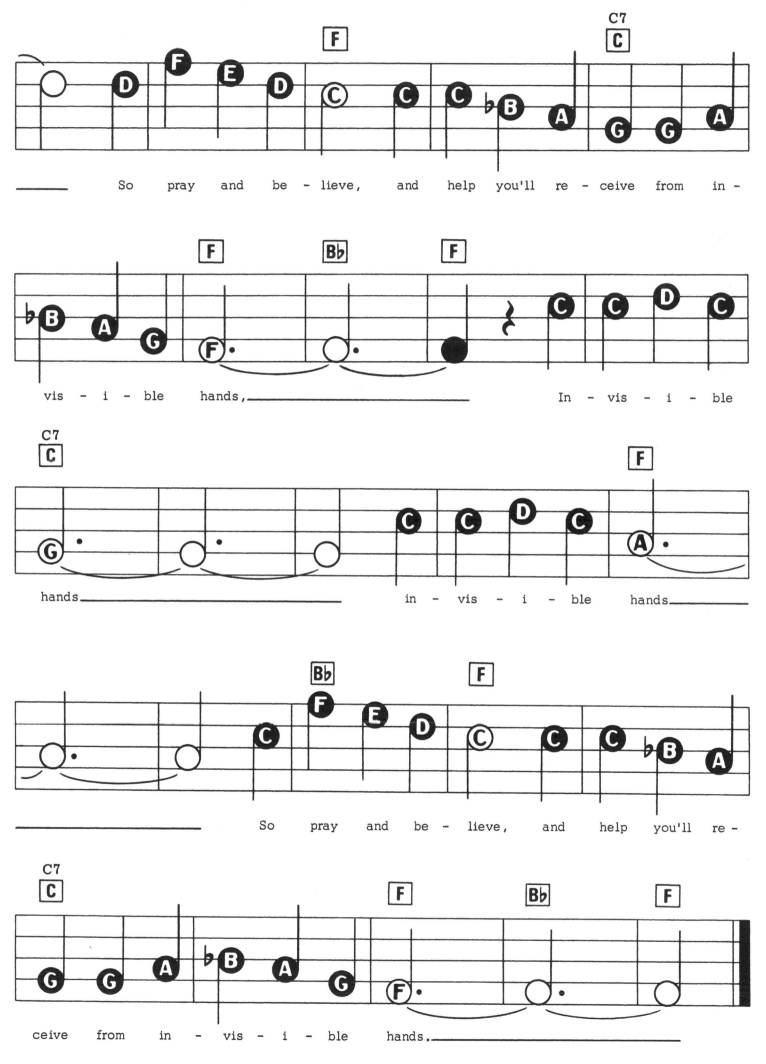

The Lily of the Valley

Registration 4
Rhythm: Fox Trot or Country

Words by Charles W. Fry
Music by William S. Hays

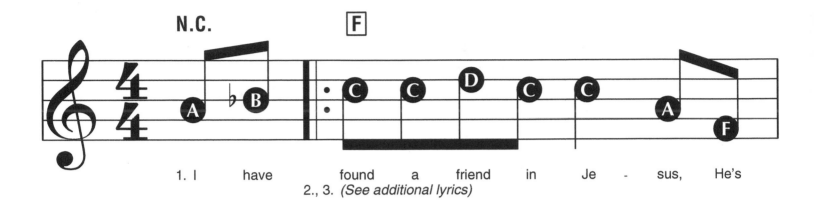

1. I have found a friend in Je - sus, He's
2., 3. *(See additional lyrics)*

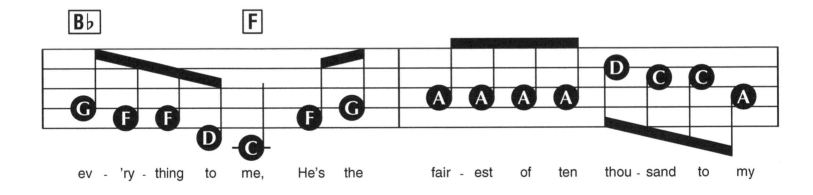

ev - 'ry - thing to me, He's the fair - est of ten thou - sand to my

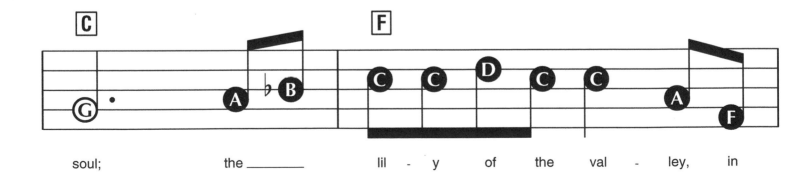

soul; the _____ lil - y of the val - ley, in

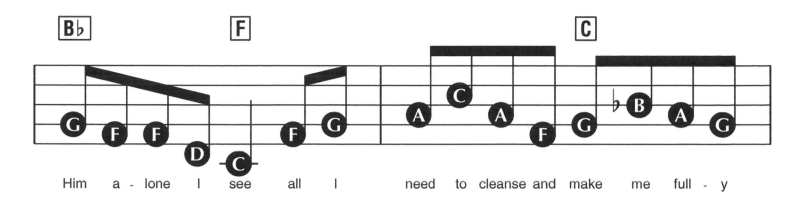

Him a - lone I see all I need to cleanse and make me full - y

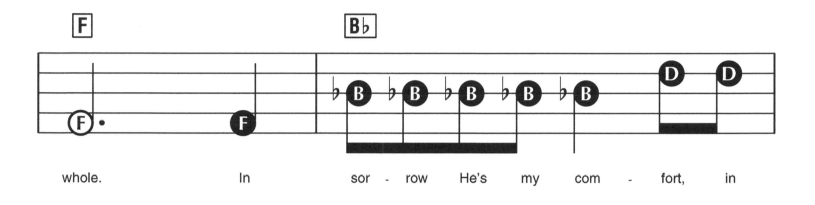

whole. In sor - row He's my com - fort, in

trou - ble He's my stay; He _____ tells me ev - 'ry care on Him to

Refrain

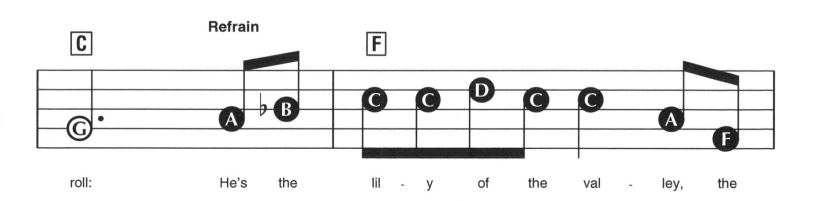

roll: He's the lil - y of the val - ley, the

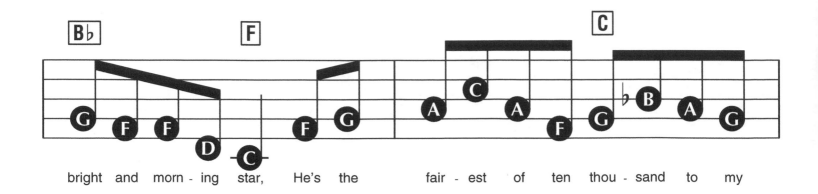

bright and morn - ing star, He's the   fair - est of ten thou - sand to my

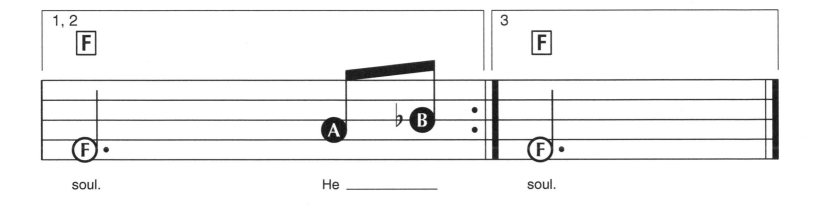

soul.   He _____ soul.

Additional Lyrics

2. He all my grief has taken, and all my sorrows borne;
   In temptation He's my strong and mighty tow'r;
   I have all for Him forsaken, and all my idols torn
   From my heart and now He keeps me by His pow'r.
   Though all the world forsake me, and Satan tempt me sore,
   Through Jesus I shall safely reach the goal:
   Refrain

3. He will never, never leave me, nor yet forsake me here,
   While I live by faith and do His blessed will;
   A wall of fire about me, I've nothing now to fear,
   With His manna He my hungry soul shall fill.
   Then sweeping up to glory to see His blessed face,
   Where rivers of delight shall ever roll:
   Refrain

Ready to Go Home

Registration 4
Rhythm: Country or Fox Trot

Words and Music by
Hank Williams

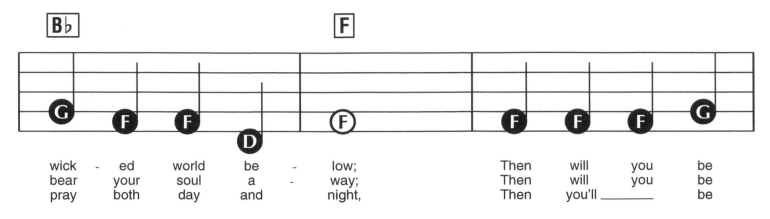

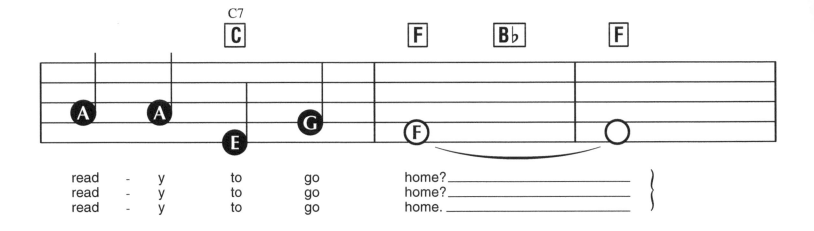

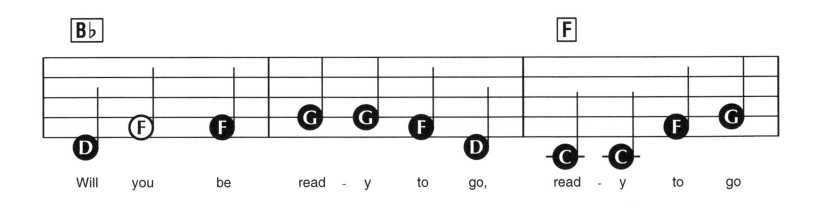

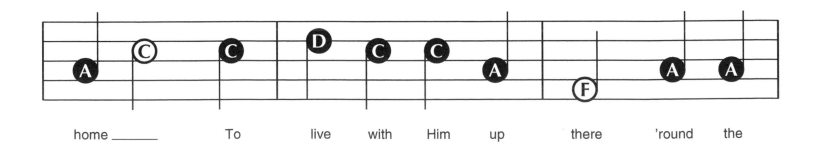

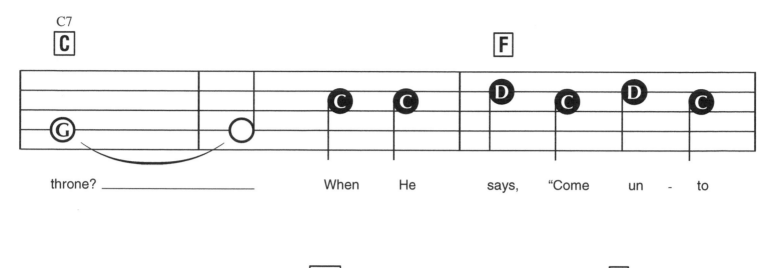

throne? _____ When He says, "Come un - to

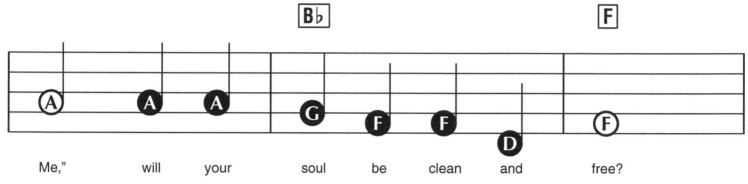

Me," will your soul be clean and free?

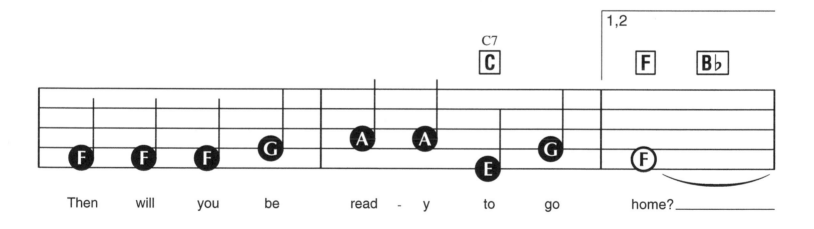

Then will you be read - y to go home? _____

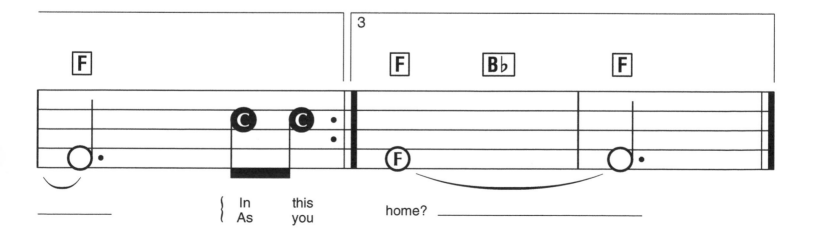

_____ In this home? _____
As you

The Love of God

Registration 1
Rhythm: Waltz

Words and Music by
Frederick M. Lehman

Mansion Over the Hilltop

Registration 4
Rhythm: Country or Swing

Words and Music by
Ira F. Stanphill

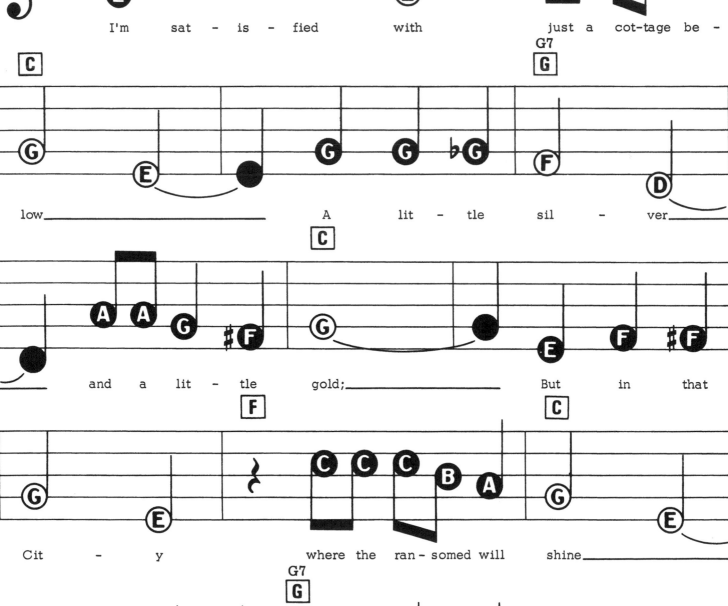

I'm sat - is - fied with just a cot-tage be - low_____ A lit - tle sil - ver_____

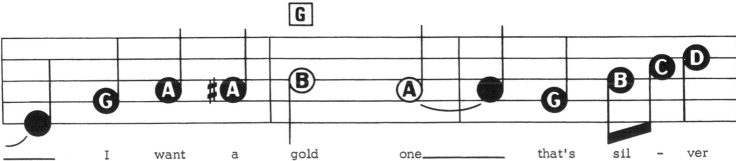

and a lit - tle gold;_____ But in that Cit - y where the ran - somed will shine_____ I want a gold one_____ that's sil - ver

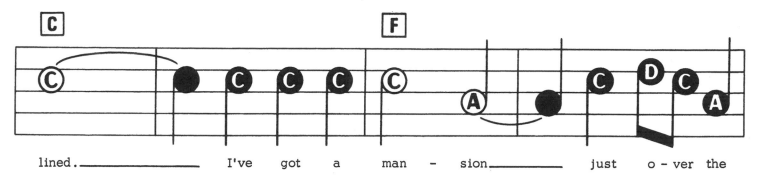

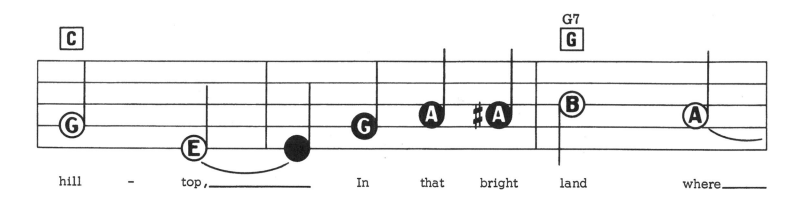

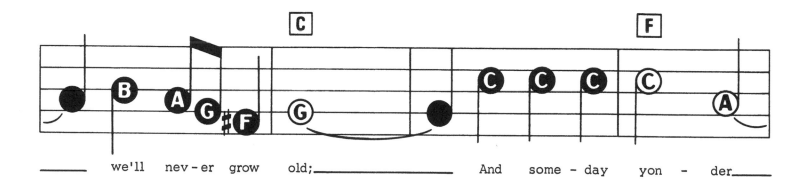

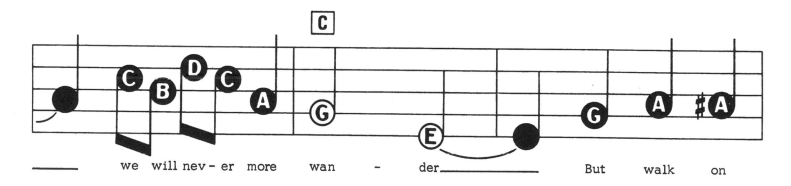

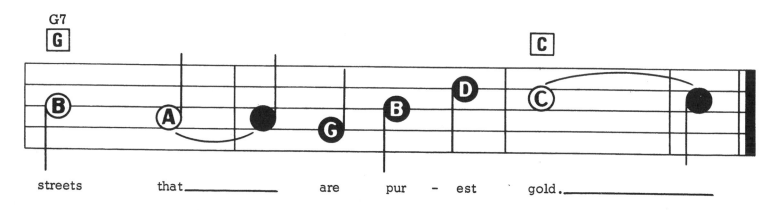

One More Valley

Registration 4
Rhythm: Country or Fox Trot

Words and Music by Jimmie Davis
and Dottie Rambo

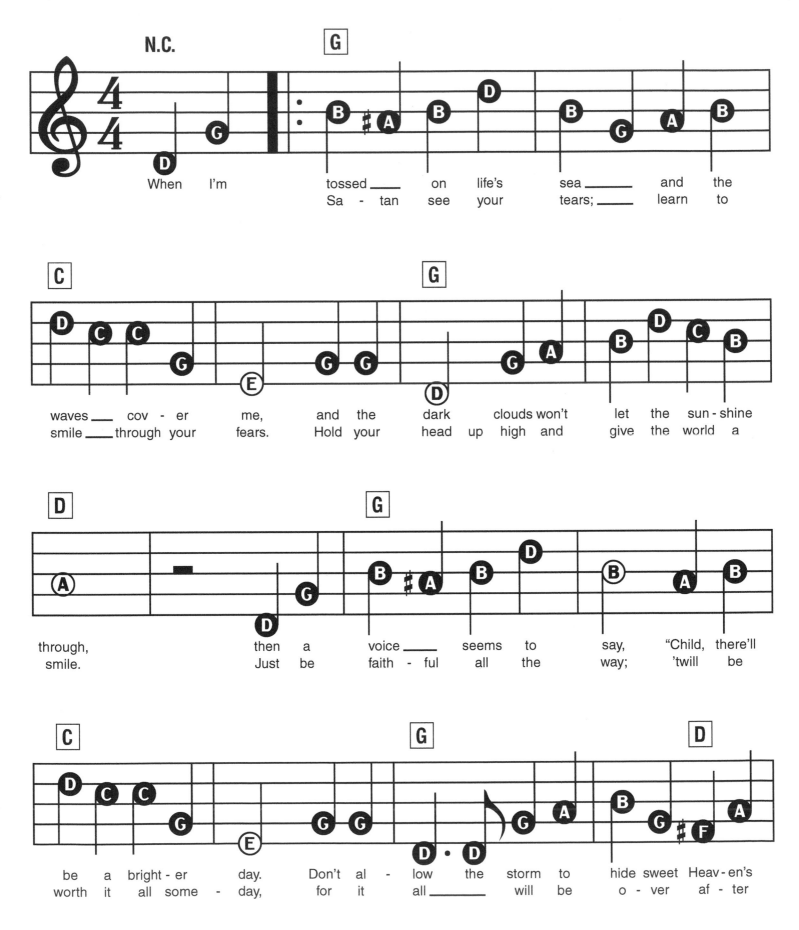

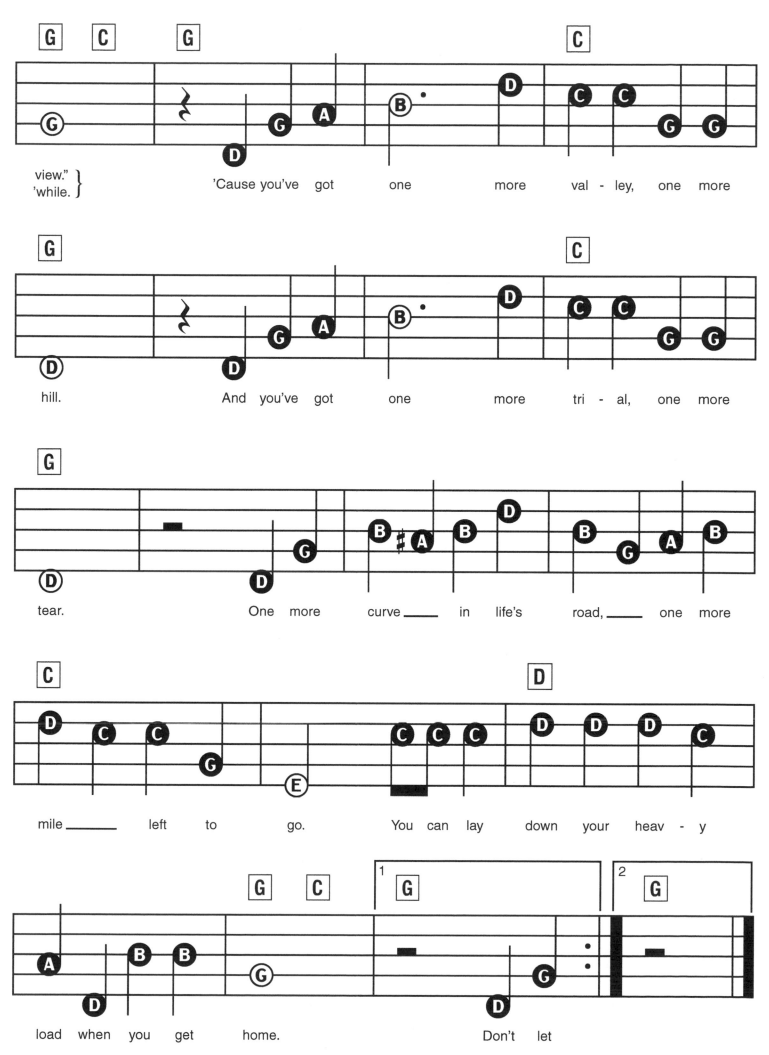

Safely in the Arms of Jesus

Registration 1
Rhythm: Country or Ballad

Words and Music by
Sonny Throckmorton

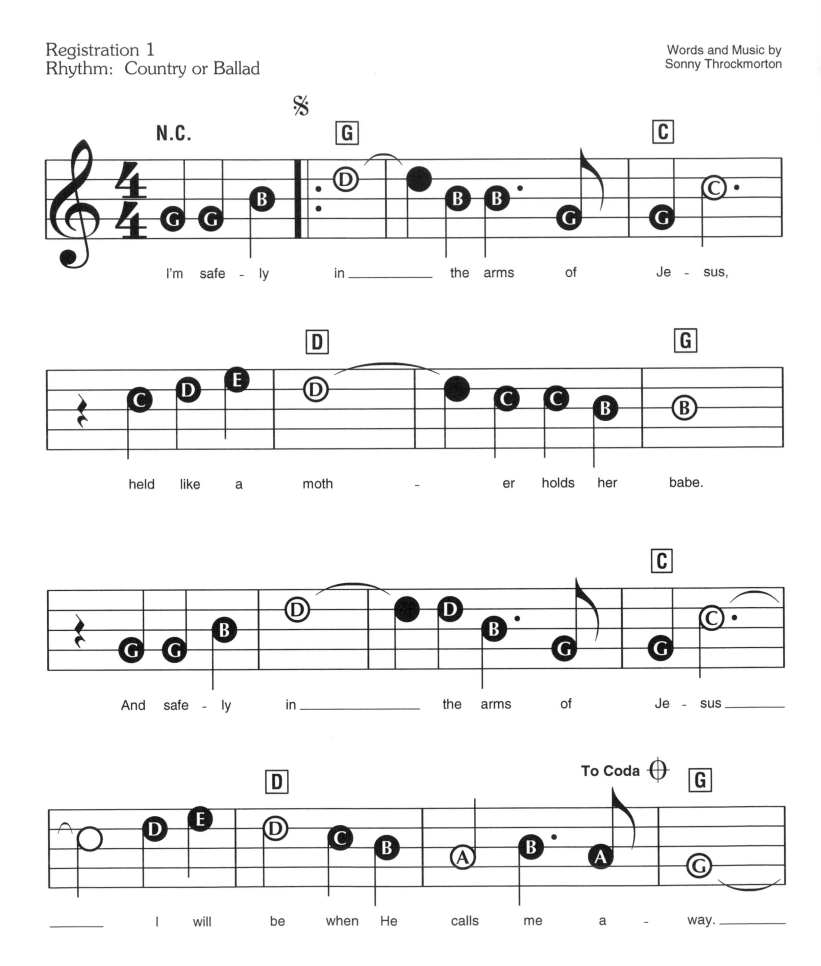

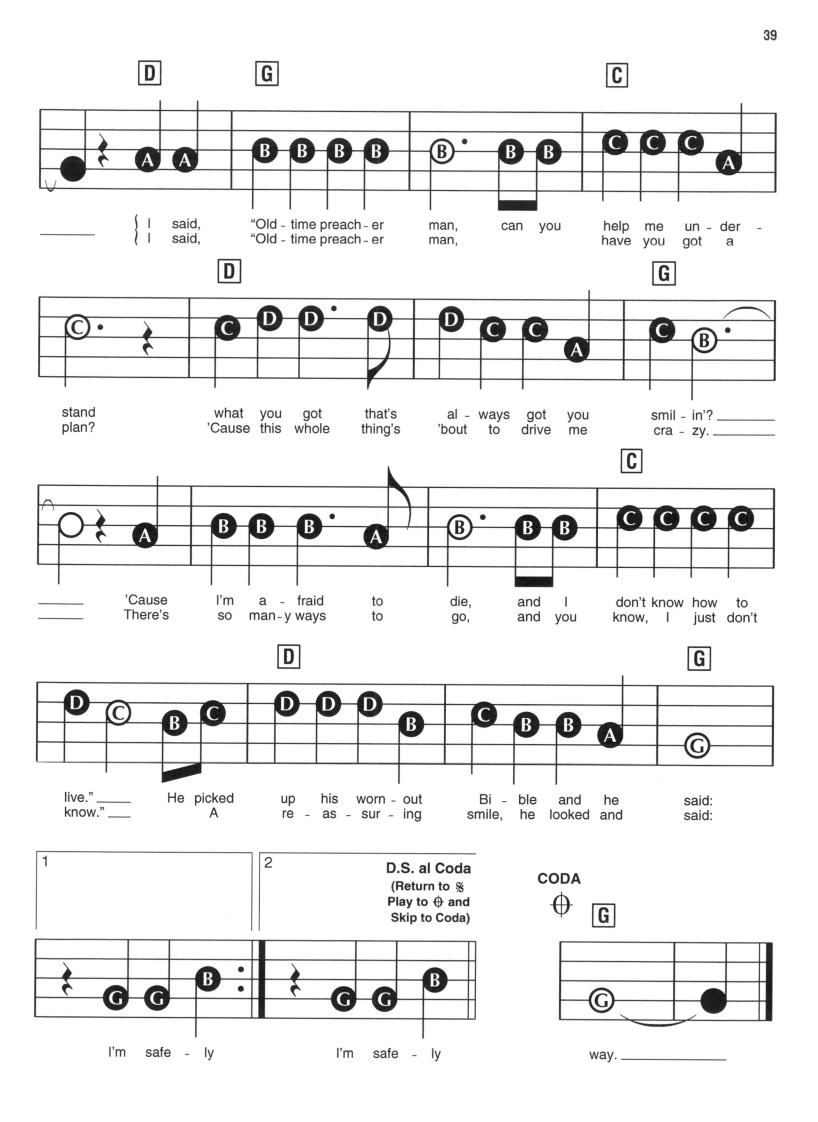

Shall We Gather at the River?

Registration 6
Rhythm: March

Words and Music by
Robert Lowry

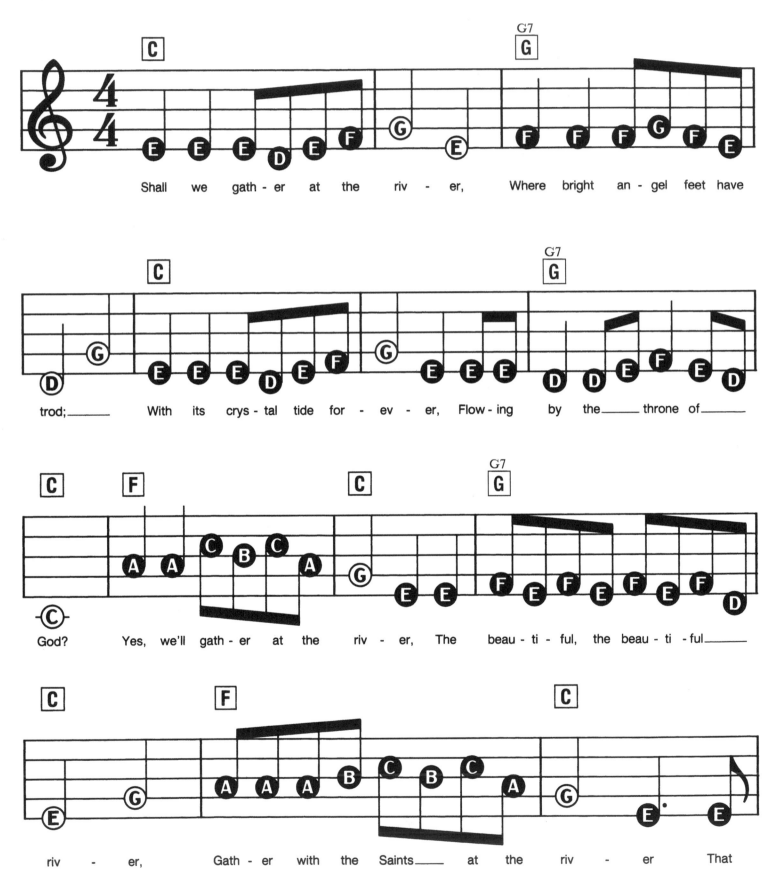

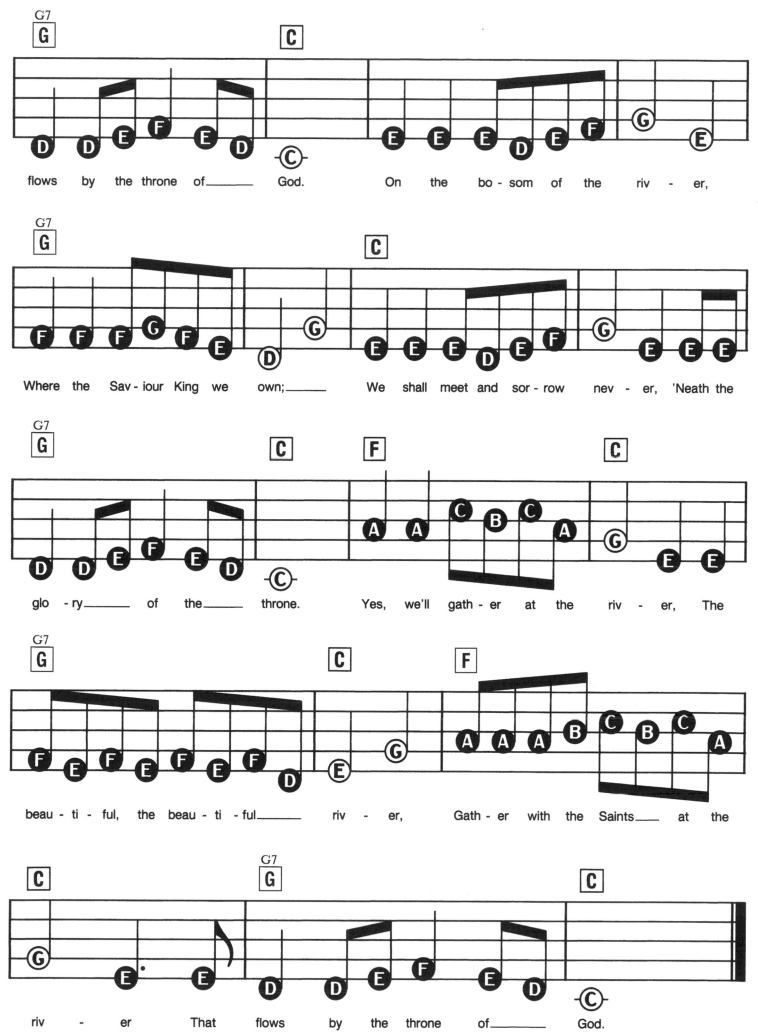

Tell It to Jesus

Registration 10
Rhythm: Ballad or Fox Trot

Words by Jeremiah E. Rankin
Music by Edmund S. Lorenz

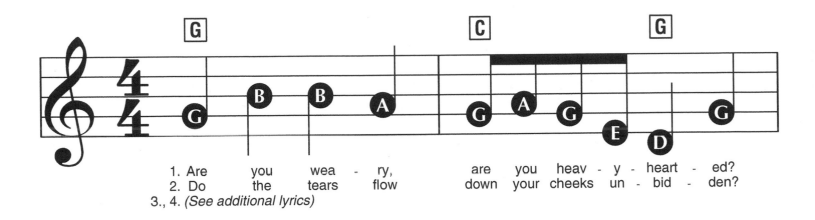

1. Are you wea - ry, are you heav - y - heart - ed?
2. Do the tears flow down your cheeks un - bid - den?
3., 4. *(See additional lyrics)*

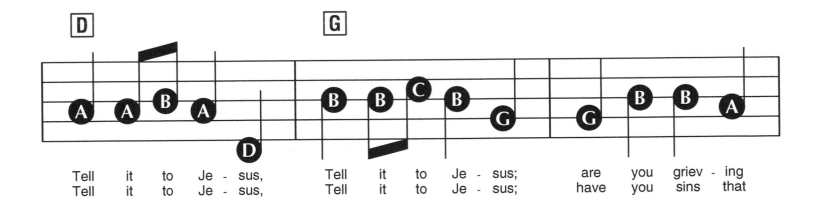

Tell it to Je - sus, Tell it to Je - sus; are you griev - ing
Tell it to Je - sus, Tell it to Je - sus; have you sins that

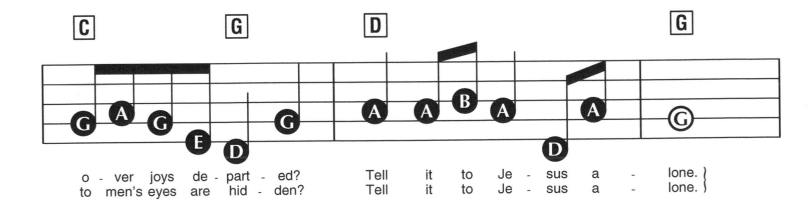

o - ver joys de - part - ed? Tell it to Je - sus a - lone.
to men's eyes are hid - den? Tell it to Je - sus a - lone.

Refrain

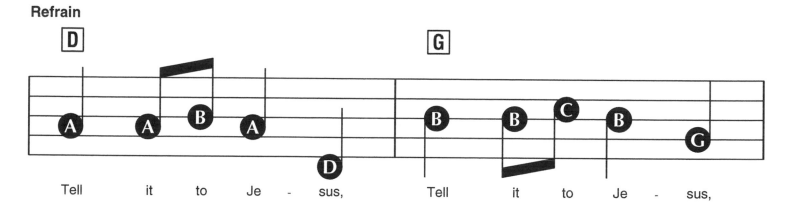

Tell it to Je - sus, Tell it to Je - sus,

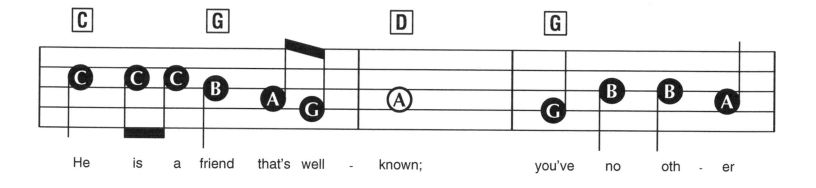

He is a friend that's well - known; you've no oth - er

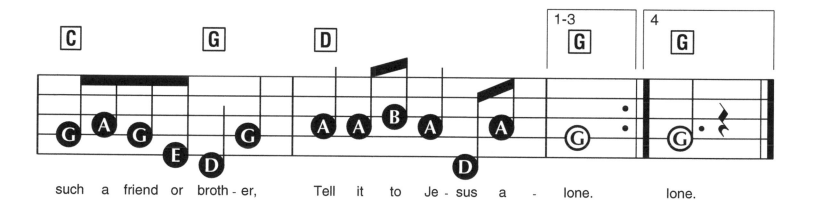

such a friend or broth - er, Tell it to Je - sus a - lone. lone.

Additional Lyrics

3. Do you fear the gath'ring clouds of sorrow?
   Tell it to Jesus, Tell it to Jesus;
   Are you anxious what shall be tomorrow?
   Tell it to Jesus alone.
   Refrain

4. Are you troubled at the thought of dying?
   Tell it to Jesus, Tell it to Jesus;
   For Christ's coming kingdom are you sighing?
   Tell it to Jesus alone.
   Refrain

Ten Thousand Angels

Registration 1
Rhythm: Ballad or 8 Beat

Words and Music by
Ray Overholt

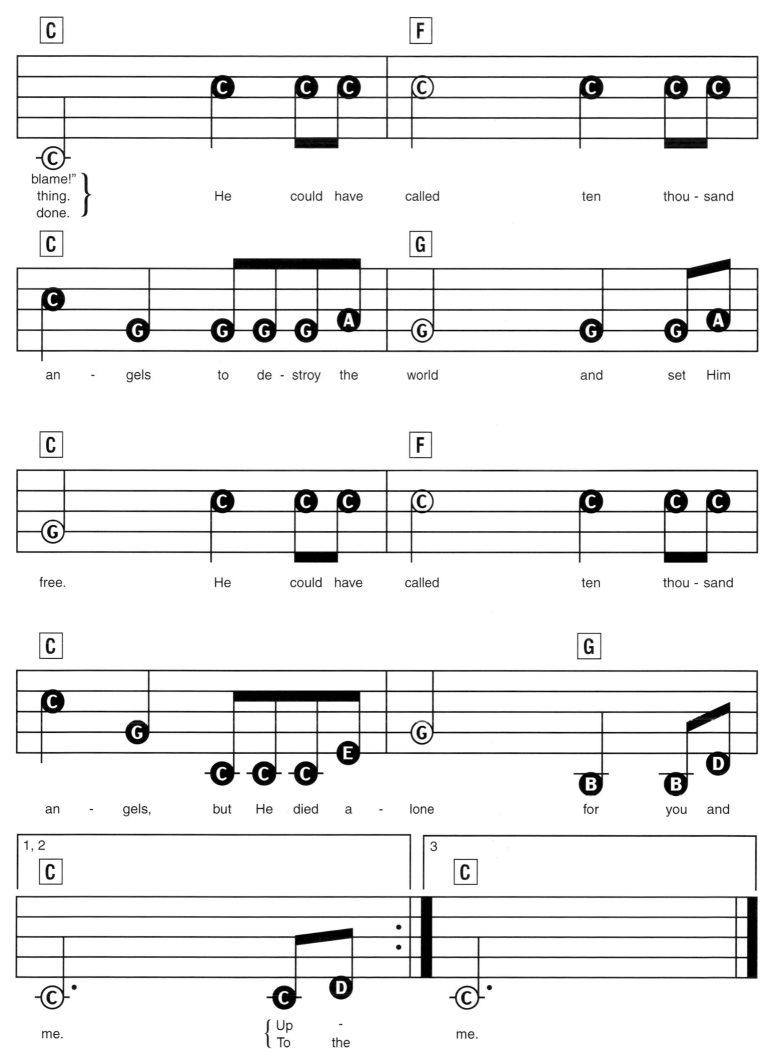

The Unclouded Day

Registration 8
Rhythm: Bluegrass

Words and Music by
J.K. Alwood

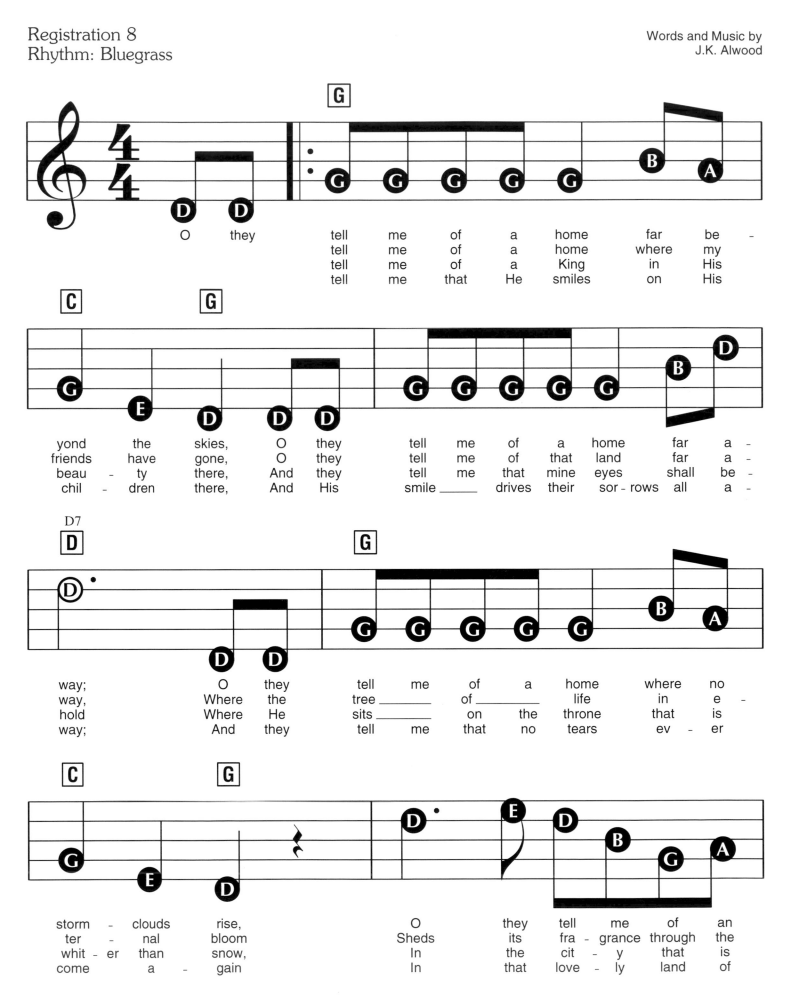

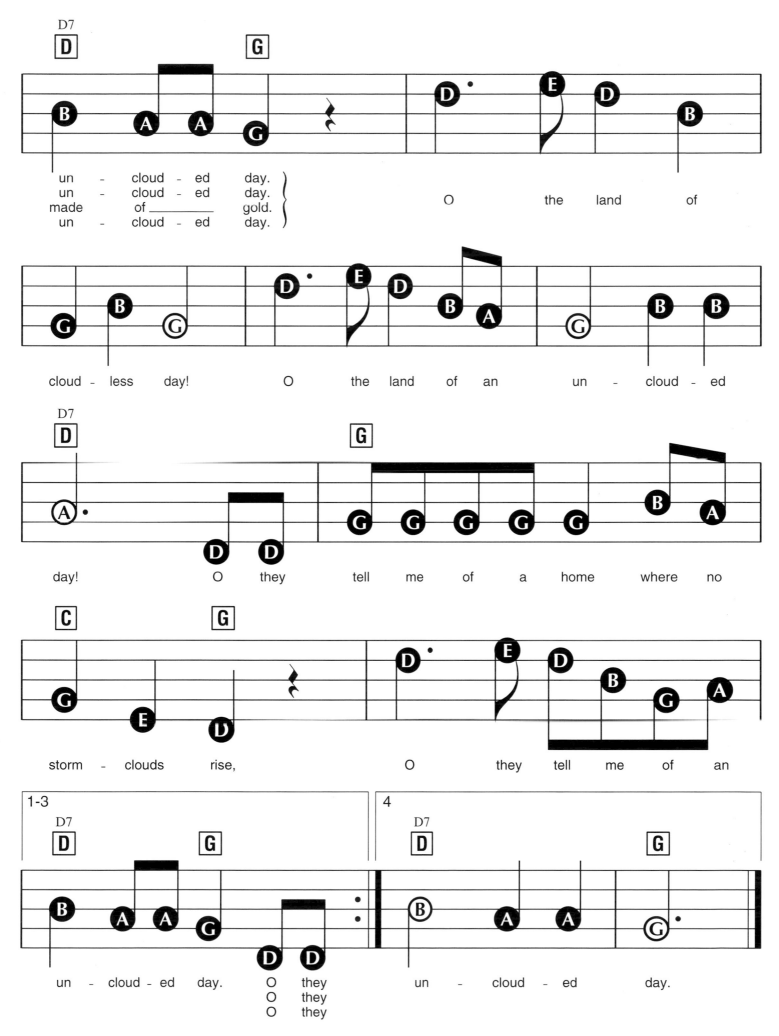